- Breah
- light the candels
- Breath
- Light the incense
- let the smoke purfy
  the space
    cast a circle

Extend your had.
  Spin clockwise
freely   wand or
              fingers

  calling the Quarters
whatchtower of the east
Element of Air, I call
  you forth to guard and
proteet this circle
  come join me now

Watch tower of the
south Element of
Fire I call you forth
~~come~~ to guard th
+protect
circle come down
me now

watch tower of the
North Element of
East I call you
forth to guard and
protect this circle
command down me
West/Water
invite deity/spirit
optional

Raise some
Energy
spin around,
dance drum sing laugh

Strech your body + smle
Direct your energy
visualy your inent
visualy your goal
stace or writedown
you vision
stace or write dow
you visen

Release / create
write draw paint
craft
Release/ create
write daw paint
craft